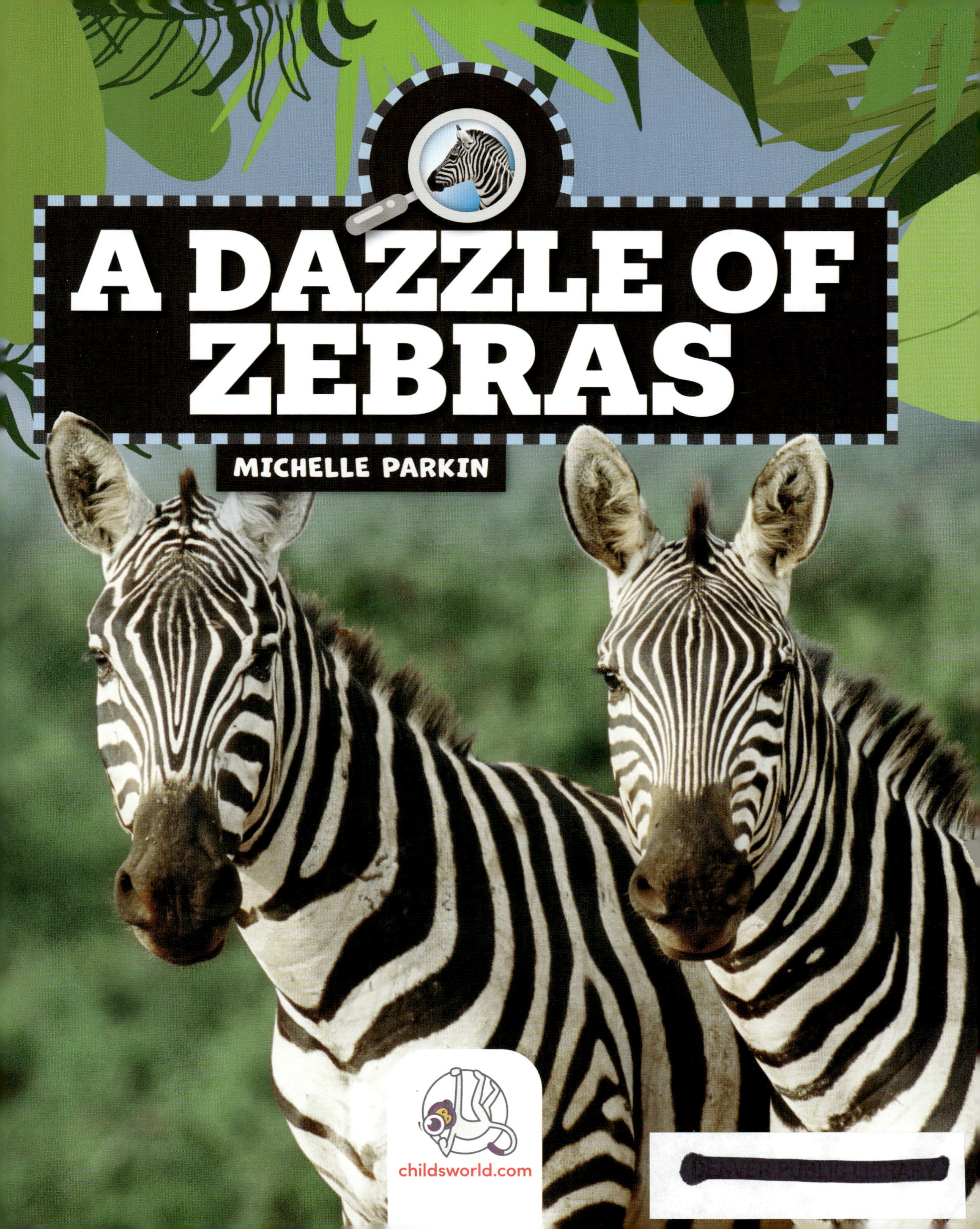
A DAZZLE OF ZEBRAS
MICHELLE PARKIN
childsworld.com

Published by The Child's World®
800-599-READ • www.childsworld.com

Photography Credits
page 1: ©Nataliya Rodina/Getty Images; page 1: ©Anastasiia Verych/Shutterstock; page 1: ©James Warwick/Getty Images; page 5: ©Wolfgang Kaehler/Contributor/Getty Images; page 11: ©Kevin Schafer/Getty Images; page 13: ©Wolfgang Kaehler/Contributor/Getty Images; page 15: ©fidanci/Getty Images; page 17: ©Gallo Images-Daryl Balfour/Getty Images; page 19: ©Bertrand Godfroid/Getty Images; page 20: ©cinoby/Getty Images; page 22: ©Dorling Kindersley: Ruth Jenkinson/Getty Images

ISBN Information
9781503885004 (Reinforced Library Binding)
9781503885837 (Portable Document Format)
9781503886476 (Online Multi-user eBook)
9781503887114 (Electronic Publication)

LCCN 2023937382

Printed in the United States of America

Michelle Parkin is an editor and children's book author. She has written more than 20 books and articles about famous people, animals, and dinosaurs. She lives with her daughter and golden retriever mix in Minnesota.

TABLE OF CONTENTS

CHAPTER 1

Meet the Dazzle

A group of zebras eats grass in the sun. Something moves in the distance. Danger is nearby! The zebras stay together. A male zebra is standing by himself a few feet away. He tilts his ears forward. Then, he makes a loud snorting sound. The speedy zebras run away. Foals run close to their mothers. Their black and white stripes blend in with one another. This makes it hard for **predators** to pick out just one zebra. The stripes also help the zebras blend into the grass. They are safe from danger.

Although they look similar, every zebra's stripes are unique.

Zebras are social animals. They don't like living alone. They live and travel in **herds**. A herd of zebras is called a dazzle. There are between 5 and 20 zebras in each dazzle. Female zebras are called mares. Males are called stallions.

Zebras live in small family dazzles. Some kinds of zebras live in dazzles of just females with their foals. Other kinds live in dazzles made up of one stallion, several mares, and their foals. These families stick together and protect each other. Male foals leave the family when they are one to three years old. They form a **bachelor** dazzle made up of all males. They will stay with this group until they are old enough to form their own family dazzle.

Zebra Size Comparison

Zebras are between 3.6 and 5.3 feet (1.1–1.5 meters) tall at their shoulders. Zebras weigh between 386 and 992 pounds (175.1–450 kilograms).

White-tailed deer stand between 3 and 4 feet (0.91–1.22 m) tall at the shoulder and weigh between 110 and 254 pounds (50–115 kg).

TIME TO EAT!

Dazzles spend most of their day **grazing**. Zebras are **herbivores**. This means they only eat plants. Zebras eat tall grass. They can also eat leaves, shrubs, twigs, and tree bark. Their teeth are made for tearing apart tough plants. Sharp front teeth bite the grass. Large back teeth crush and grind the food.

There are three types of zebras. All of them live in Africa. Plains zebras live on grasslands in eastern and southern Africa. Mountain zebras live in hilly, dry areas in southwest Africa, Namibia, and southwestern Angola. Grevy's zebras live in Ethiopia and northern Kenya. Plains zebras are the most common. They are the zebras people usually see in zoos. No matter where they're from, all zebras live in dazzles.

Dazzles sometimes combine to form large groups to search for food. These are called superherds. Superherds can have tens of thousands of zebras! But the zebras will still stick with their smaller family dazzles as they travel. The superherds can also include other animals, such as antelopes and wildebeests. They travel thousands of miles to find green grass and fresh water.

CHAPTER 2

All in the Family

Female plains and mountain zebras only **mate** with the stallion who leads their dazzle. Male Grevy's zebras find females that are ready to mate. Then they leave. Twelve months later, the female will give birth to a baby zebra. They have just one baby, but sometimes they have twins.

Foals can stand 10 to 20 minutes after birth. They can walk and run after one hour. For the first few days, the mother and her foal live separate from their dazzle. This is so the baby can learn what its mother's stripes look like. From then on, it will be able to follow her wherever she goes. It can also find her if they get separated. When they are about two years old, young zebras leave their dazzles. Females join another dazzle. Males join bachelor dazzles.

Zebras usually have just one baby. A baby zebra is called a foal.

CHAPTER 3

Who's in Charge?

A stallion is in charge of the dazzle. He travels at the back of the herd and keeps an eye out for danger. After the stallion, the oldest mare is in charge. She travels at the front of the dazzle. Like the stallion, she watches for any danger. She decides where the dazzle will go. She gets to eat and drink before all of the other mares. If other mares try to drink before her, she will chase them away.

The mares stay in the same dazzle for their entire lives. If their stallion dies, another male will replace him. Sometimes a younger stallion challenges the older one. He rears up on his hind legs and kicks. The two stallions fight, biting and kicking each other. Sometimes the females will help to defend their stallion. If the younger stallion wins, the older stallion has to leave. Then the younger one takes over the dazzle.

Male zebras are slightly larger than females.

Predators such as African wild dogs, cheetahs, leopards, lions, hyenas, and crocodiles hunt dazzles. Zebras use their sharp eyesight to protect themselves during both the day and night. When dazzles eat, they stand facing different directions so nothing can sneak up on them. The dazzle doesn't all sleep at once. They take turns so there is always a lookout. Zebras also sleep standing up to stay safe.

Whenever danger is near, dazzles try to run away. They can run very fast. Zebras' stripes make it confusing for predators to look at them. But sometimes, running isn't possible. If a predator gets too close, the dazzle forms a half circle. They all face the predator, ready to fight. Zebras have a strong bite. Their back legs can deliver powerful and deadly kicks. If a zebra gets hurt, others in the dazzle will try to drive the predator away from the injured animal.

Zebras gallop like horses and use their long, thin legs to run away from danger.

CHAPTER 4

What Makes Dazzles Unique?

Zebras look a lot like horses. They have pointed ears. They walk on **hooved** feet. Zebras are **related** to horses and donkeys. But zebras have black bodies covered with white stripes. A zebra's stripes are like a fingerprint. No two patterns are alike. Zebras recognize each other's stripes. It's how foals follow their mothers.

Dazzles communicate with each other through sounds. They bray loudly like donkeys. They also bark and snort. Zebras use their ears, eyes, and mouths to send messages as well. If a zebra's ears are flat and lie back, it can mean, "Watch out! Danger!"

Zebras often travel with other animals, such as wildebeests. There is safety in numbers!

MYSTERY STRIPES

Scientists have many ideas about why zebras have stripes. Some believe all the stripes in a dazzle protect them from predators. The stripes from a dazzle of zebras blend together. Predators are not able to pick out one zebra to chase. Other scientists think the stripes control a zebra's body temperature. Still others think a zebra's stripes keep biting insects, such as horseflies, away.

Why Dazzles Matter

Dazzles face many dangers. Grevy's zebras are **endangered**. But all three types of zebras are at risk. **Poachers** kill zebras for their coats and meat. There are still many plains zebras and mountain zebras. But that can easily change.

One type of zebra is already **extinct**. It was called the quagga. It had stripes on its head, shoulders, and back. The rest of it was brown. It was closely related to the plains zebra. Humans hunted it for its skin. The last one died in 1872. If people are not careful, the same thing could happen to the zebras we still have.

Zebras' unique stripes make them a common target for poachers.

Zebra dazzles are important to our world. They graze on grass, leaves, and plants as they travel. This grazing removes old plants and makes way for new plant growth. Zebras are also a source of food for other animals. They are needed to keep other animals thriving.

Groups such as the African Wildlife Foundation work to protect zebras. They work with African governments. One of the things they do is create wildlife **corridors**. People can't build there. These are safe places for dazzles of zebras to travel. This lets the dazzles move between protected areas so they can travel to find food. Hopefully zebras will be around to dazzle us for many years to come.

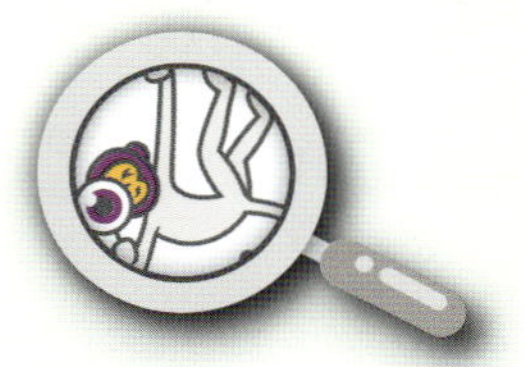

Wonder More

Wondering about New Information

After reading this book, did you learn something new about zebra dazzles? List three facts you found interesting.

Wondering How It Matters

Plains zebras are often found in zoos. Have you ever seen a zebra dazzle at the zoo? If you have, describe what it was like to see a dazzle up close. If you haven't, describe what you think it would be like.

Wondering Why

All three types of zebras are at risk. Why do you think zebras are important? How would the world be different if they died out?

Ways to Keep Wondering

What questions do you still have about dazzles of zebras? Where can you learn more about them?

Make Your Own Zebra Dazzle

Make your own dazzle of zebras with this crafting project you can do at home.

What You Need:

- Three empty paper towel rolls
- Black marker
- Glue
- Scissors
- Pencil
- Three sheets of white construction paper

Steps to Take:

1. Glue white construction paper onto each of the five toilet paper rolls. These are the zebras' bodies.
2. Flatten the other two toilet paper rolls and cut them into 1/2 inch strips. You will have a total of 16 strips. These are the zebras' legs.
3. Using a pencil, draw three zebra heads and three zebra tails on a piece of white paper. Carefully cut them out.
4. With your black marker, draw stripes, a mane, eyes, a nose, and a mouth on each zebra head. Draw stripes on each zebra's body. Add stripes and hooves to the legs, too!
5. Put a zebra head into the slits at the front of each body. Put the legs into the four slits on the bottom of each body. DAZZLE your family with your zebra creations!

Glossary

bachelor (BATCH-uh-lur) A bachelor is a male human or animal who does not have a partner.

corridors (KOR-ih-dors) Corridors are narrow pieces of land that connect two larger areas.

endangered (en-DAYN-jurd) Endangered animals, plants, or other living things are at risk of dying out.

extinct (ek-STINGKT) Extinct animals, plants, or other living things have completely disappeared from Earth.

grazing (GRAYZ-ing) Grazing animals eat grass growing in the field.

herbivores (HUR-buh-vorz) Herbivores are animals that eat plants rather than other animals.

herds (HURDZ) A herd is a large group of the same type of animal that live and travel together.

hooved (HOOVD) Hooved animals have hard coverings called hooves over their feet.

mate (MAYT) When animals mate, they come together to produce offspring.

poachers (POH-churz) Poachers are people who hunt and kill animals illegally.

predators (PRED-uh-turz) Predators are animals that live by hunting other animals for food.

related (reh-LAY-tid) Animals that are related are part of the same animal family.

Find Out More

In the Library

Brandle, Marie. *Zebra Foals in the Wild.* Minneapolis, MN: Jump!, Inc., 2023.

Maloney, Brenna. *Horse or Zebra.* New York, NY: Children's Press, 2023.

Riggs, Kate. *Zebras.* North Mankato, MN: The Creative Company, 2022.

On the Web

Visit our website for links about zebra dazzles:
childsworld.com/links

Note to Parents, Caregivers, Teachers, and Librarians: We routinely verify our web links to make sure they are safe and active sites. So encourage your readers to check them out!

Index